FIND

WHY!

To become *Frickin'* Awesome

W♥men
only

Choose a life of freedom and take back control

Cheryl Chapman

Orders: Please contact Amazon.co.uk

You can also order via Cheryl@cheryl-chapman.com

ISBN: 978-0-9934587-0-5

First published 2015

Printed in Great Britain for Cheryl Chapman by Bell & Bain Ltd, 303 Burnfield Road, Thornliebank, Glasgow G46 7UQ

CONTENTS

ACKNOWLEGEMENTS

Thank you to my parents, who did the best they could for me, who loved me and tried to keep me safe.

Thank you to my sister Gemma (I was an only child for 15 years and 11 months and then you arrived and my inheritance halved – joking ☺), thank you for being there for me and providing me with an amazing nephew Leon (who will be a professional footballer – watch this space).

To my husband Mr C, my rock, who has always supported me by allowing me to follow my WHY! You are one in a million – Love You.

A special mention to My Staffordshire Bull Terrier 'Ozzy Dog', who sat at my feet whilst I wrote these words

To Marion who helped me to become carefree.

Finally, Thank you to YOU, that's right YOU. You know who you are ☺.

You played a big part of my life by either supporting me, pushing me, inspiring me and sometimes even pissing me off (I now know that was because I let you). I hope that you are happy and living your WHY!

"Beauty begins the moment you decide to be yourself"

Coco Chanel

PREFACE

This book is based on 9 Pearls of Wisdom:

Pearl 1

You are the only person who can control the way you feel.

Blaming others for how you feel is giving away your power – making you a passive victim. By learning how to respond, and not react, you can take back your power and become actively responsible for YOU. This will allow you to take control of yourself and your feelings.

Pearl 2

You can't change anyone else.

Become aware of things that you cannot change, such as other people's opinions and behaviour. If people are beyond your influence then don't waste your energy. No matter how hard you try, they won't change.

You can be the juiciest, ripest cherry possible, but the reality is that some people will always hate cherries.

Pearl 3

Your past is your past.

All of the pain, frustration and sadness that you have experienced in your life has brought you to the place where you are now, and made you the person we see today. These experiences have shaped you and served you.

You can choose to keep living in the past, or move forward towards your future.

Pearl 4

You are what you think.

Whether you are a daughter, sister, friend, lover, wife, mother or grandmother – you have thoughts. Energy goes where attention flows. Thoughts become words, words become behaviour, behaviours become habits, habits become values and values become destiny.

Surround yourselves with others that want the same things as you.

Pearl 5

Before you start your journey, you need to know where you are now.

Just like a satellite navigation system in a car, you need to know where your starting point is before any journey can begin. Discovering where you are consciously, and unconsciously, will help you to pinpoint your current life location.

Pearl 6

You must be clear on what it is that you want.

One day you will die – FACT!

You must decide what you want to happen in your life – don't leave it to chance.

The difference between successful people and unsuccessful people, is that successful people KNOW what they want, and go after it! Unsuccessful people do not.

Pearl 7

You can have the life you want, but you have to take action.

The Law Of Attraction has two equally important parts. The first part is the ability to attract, and the 2nd part is that you NEED to take action. As Einstein once said, "Insanity isn't doing the same thing every day, it's doing the same thing every day and expecting something to change."

If you change nothing, nothing changes.

Pearl 8

You need to FIND YOUR WHY.

Without a WHY life will just happen to you, you'll die with regrets.

When you find your WHY, you'll be motivated, full of energy, living your life on purpose, satisfied, happy and fulfilled.

You will be a role model to others and inspire them to find their WHY too.

Pearl 9

You can make these changes, even if right now you don't know how. In this book, I will provide you with a step-by-step plan. This plan will help you to take back control of your life, so that you can LIVE – LOVE – LAUGH every day; all in your own unique way.

If you can see and feel a connection with any of these Pearls of Wisdom, now is the time to invest in yourself and begin the next chapter of your life.

Additionally, if you know anyone within your network of friends and family who might also be interested in these pearls, please let them know so they too can benefit from the content of this life-changing book.

With love,

Cheryl

Cheryl Chapman

But before we begin our journey together, there is something I think you might want to know ...

PROLOGUE

It's November 2013 and I'm lying on my back in the middle of a room in Angel Islington. It's been over 40 minutes, and I can hear my stomach rumbling.

Leaning over me, I can see her fiddling with her papers and workbook. The room is filled with every kind of clutter. A hammock, hand drawn etchings on the wall, piles of books and foreign trinkets; you name it, she's got it. She is the female version of Indiana Jones, in search of a thousand ancient truths.

As she speaks, it's like Cilla Black has arrived in the room, "Ok Cheryl, put your hand up and try to resist. Mmmm...yes. Ok, and again."

As I watch her in her flowing orange, white and burgundy hippy frock, she drops some papers on the floor, and as her red glasses slip to the end of her nose, I can't help thinking, "Bless her – I don't think she's mastered this yet, but she's a friend and she asked me to help her. I'll just lie here, I'm sure it will all be over soon."

Little did I know what was about to happen...

"Ok Cheryl, with the information I'm picking up on, it is either you have to watch the energy you give to others

(As she is pointing to her book, I'm thinking, "This is a crock of shit!")

Or, it's you have to be careful?"

"OH MY GOD, THEY'VE FOUND OUT!" The voice is my head is loud and scared. My stomach starts to somersault. Finally, the tears start to flow. My mind goes back to when I was 5 years old, "But WHY, Mummy?"

This is where it all started.

CHAPTER 1

CAN YOU KEEP A SECRET?

Can you remember a time when you were a child?

Can you remember the questions you used to ask all the time?

Why? Why? Why?

Why are there stars in the sky?

Why is the sun yellow?

But why do I have to wear this pink dress?

That's right, a child's most used word is WHY!

If you'd been with me in October 1969, you would have witnessed a time when that question was the number one thing on my mind.

Picture the scene. I'm standing in an army quarters hallway. My mother, swinging sixties high hair and short skirt, is wrapping a silver chain around my neck. On the end of it is a key.

"Can you keep a secret, Cheryl? Mummy needs you to keep a secret. You can't tell anyone about this key – I need you to keep it hidden until you come home and then use it to let yourself in, can you do this for Mummy?"

"But why, Mummy?"

"Cheryl, Daddy is away with the other soldiers and Mummy needs to work, so I won't be here when you come home. But you're a big girl now, so you will be fine until I get back. Remember you've got to be careful, don't tell anyone. Don't let anyone in, or Mummy might get into trouble and you might not see her again."

At first it was fine. I would run around the flat, bounce on the settee and eat as much ice cream as I wanted... but when it got dark I would hide under the blanket on my bed, and pray that my mummy would come home soon.

I'd like to tell you that this was the only time I was asked to wear the key. Unfortunately this happened almost every day, from the age of 5, throughout my childhood. Have you ever thought about how your upbringing influences your adult life? For me it wasn't until I got older that some other elements of being an 'army brat' started to appear.

Me & my mum (I told you her skirt was short)

Are you a Gypsy?

It's August 2011 and I'm sitting with my friend Toria (she looks like Angelina Jolie) in Bettys Tea Room in York, England. Bettys is one of those quintessentially British establishments that is steeped in history and has been around since 1919.

Personally, I love it for the heart shape cakes.

"So Chez, (that's what all my friends call me) how's the job?"

"Oh you know, same shit – different day, I think it's time for a move!"

Looking at her watch, Toria says, "Oh yeah that will be about right, you've been there 2 years and so this is when you get itchy feet. Why do you think you constantly want to move? Are you a gypsy?"

With a dismissive tone, I start to recall the list of jobs that I've had recently. I started enthusiastically imagining she's got it wrong – only to find out she's right ...22 months, 24 months, 2 years and nearly 2 years again!

"Well Toria, it's because my dad was in the army. We used to move every 2 years – clearly it's in my blood. Besides, sometimes I just don't feel like I fit in."

"Chez, maybe you should have a change in your career instead of just moving from one place to another, experiencing the same problems? For someone who thinks they don't fit in, you're great with people. Maybe you should consider being a counsellor?"

"You are joking right? I'm too old to make any changes now. I've been working in retail for over 25 years, how the hell could I do anything different?"

I also had a secret that I couldn't let anyone know about.

My best friends

Maybe it was because I couldn't get excited about my job, or maybe because my husband was away from home a lot...whatever it was, I found myself spending every weekend with two of my favourite friends: Gordon & Stella.

Let me tell you about Gordon and Stella. Gordon had wide shoulders and a white cap, and a way of helping me feel numb. Stella...well, she just made me feisty. Together, they had the ability to help me forget all my troubles. That's right, if you haven't guessed it by now − I was a binge drinker, with a terrible 'thank god it's Friday' habit. Friday evening began with Gordon's Gin and tins of Stella Artois, and didn't end until the hangover kicked in the next morning. Sometimes it didn't end till Saturday night or Sunday morning.

It was when Monday arrived that the sober truth became apparent. I felt trapped. Trapped in a job I hated, trapped by the debt that I'd accrued as

I bought things designed to make me feel better, to distract me from the reality of the life I'd created. I hated my life. I was fat, frumpy and heading towards 50. I was living a lie. And worse still, I believed there was nothing that could be done.

Then, in October 2011, something happened that completely changed my life forever.

Recruiting for my funeral

If you had been with me on the 15th October 2011, you would have seen me sitting inside The Troxy in London, a large art deco theatre with two sweeping staircases. It was the type of theatre that would have been perfect for the likes of Fred Astaire and Ginger Rogers, but it wasn't dancers that took to the stage that day. On that day, it was speakers.

"Who's this?" said the Indian lady sitting next to me

"Not sure, but he looks small!"

"Ladies and gentlemen, please welcome to the stage... MR ANDY HARRINGTON!"

The audience were clapping and cheering. I wondered if I was in the right place. This was a far cry from my everyday life.

As Andy started his presentation, it was as if he was talking just to me.

"If you were to die tomorrow, who would mourn your loss?"

Turning to the Indian lady next to me, I announced, "Well I've got 43 friends on Facebook, so I guess not many." Then, as if an arrow had been fired into my heart, I heard the words:

"If the number is low, it means you've lead a life of insignificance."

Have you ever had a time when someone spoke to you and you felt like you had a deep connection with them, as if they were on the same wavelength? Well, that was what happened to me that day. So when Andy presented the opportunity to attend the Public Speakers University, I ran straight to the back of the room. I just knew that this guy was going to help me. Maybe you could call it woman's intuition, but whatever it was, I was hooked. After the PSU I was invited to join The Professional Speakers Academy (PSA) and continued to work with Andy as my mentor. I still wasn't really sure what I was doing – but I was certain that it was the right thing.

Back at work, my boss sensed that something was happening...

"Cheryl, it seems like this speaking is of more interest to you than your role here. Your role here should come first, this is how you make a living! You need to choose which you want to carry on with."

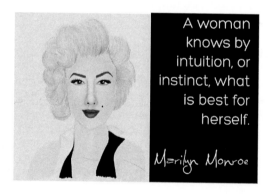

A woman knows by intuition, or instinct, what is best for herself.

Marilyn Monroe

Have you ever known with all your heart what you should do, and what the right thing is to do, but before you can do it your head kicks in?

"You have a mortgage to pay, Cheryl. What about all the debt you have, what about your responsibilities?"

I spent the next few days in turmoil. I knew I couldn't speak to my family about it because I didn't want them to worry, so instead I talked to myself.

"What should I do – should I stay on the track that I know so well, with the safety of a salary and a company car, or should I change direction and choose a life that could give me a purpose?"

What would you do?

It was at that time that a friend from The Professional Speakers Academy asked me if I would be a case study for her Kinesiology course. Marion said it could help me to understand which direction to take. I have to admit I didn't really understand what it was, but by now I was desperate!

You have to be careful

Let's return to Angel Islington. There I was, lying on my back, with tears streaming down my face.

"Cheryl, does "you have to be careful" mean something to you?"

"Yes, Marion it does – I understand now that I've tried to be careful all my life. I've tried to do what's best for everyone else, but so far this has just led to me being unhappy and feeling like I don't fit in. But if I'm not careful, what do I do? I've spent my whole life being careful!"

It was with Marion's help that I began to see that there was an alternative way to live my life. And so I resigned from my job to follow my purpose, to find my WHY.

It was tough at first. My family thought I'd gone mad. I lost my salary overnight, and my financial situation was dire to say the least.

However, it suddenly felt like I'd got my life back. I felt motivated, and had the time and the energy to make a complete change in direction. I studied NLP: Life Coaching. I implemented all of the tools, tips and the techniques and my client base started to build. I wrote my first book, The Devil, The Angel and YOU, to help others to recognise the voices in their head.

My client base continued to grow, and as I shared more and more success with them, my confidence began to grow too. I used to think I didn't fit in. I used to think that I was the only one who felt so lost, who wondered if this is all there is to life, but now I know that I was not alone. So many women live like that, and now I can help them to choose a life of freedom. I know what it's like to feel trapped, and I wouldn't wish this on anyone else in the world.

"The 2 most important days in your life are the day you were born & the day you find out WHY"

Mark Twain

Speaking to an audience in Singapore 2014

Speaking at Queens of Life in Warsaw 2015

Today I travel all over the world sharing a message of hope and help to large groups of people. In the last 2 years I have spoken on stages in Australia, Malaysia, Singapore, Thailand, South Africa, Europe and Canada.

Appearing on Slovenian TV 2014

I was awarded the Trainer of the Year award by Andy Harrington, the man who helped me to realise I had a gift inside me.

Today I am renowned as one of the Top Speaker Coaches in the World, mentoring thousands of clients internationally.

Joining the Professional Speakers Academy in 2012 and Receiving Trainer of the year award from my mentor Andy Harrington in 2015.

I launched Cheryl C TV earlier this year and created The Law of Action with Marion, who helped me to become aware of and then clear my unconscious blocks. At the Law of Action, our mission is to help you 'Find your WHY'.

Sharing my WHY!

Me & Marion (The female Indiana Jones)

Why do I do this?

For some reason I'd stopped questioning, and stopped asking "why?" as I got older and just accepted what life gave me. Have you done that too? If so, maybe it's because we were told the answer is, "it's because it just is!"

However, now I believe we should never stop asking. I believe we should never stop trying. Never stop, until you FIND your WHY!

My WHY is helping others to CHOOSE A LIFE OF FREEDOM!

Live, Love & Laugh every day, By being unique in your own special way.

Cheryl Chapman

Now it's your turn

In the coming chapters, I will reveal how you can go from having a lack of belief in yourself and being easily distracted; to being aware of where you are right now. With my advice, you can set your intentions for the future, and manifest the life you want, by finding your personal WHY.

So let's get started. It's going to be a big dipper of a ride, so fasten yourself in and get ready to scream with excitement!

"After almost 25 years of talking on TV every day, my most profound and meaningful memories are of people getting to see the light inside themselves, and having an aha moment. Over the years all my teaching on the show has taught me. I've been strengthened by the sharing of it, and I know for sure as I move into the next chapter of my life and career: Teaching will hold an even greater place. It's what I'm called to do. We're all called. If you are breathing, you have a contribution to make to our human community. The real work of your life is to figure out your function-your part in the whole-as soon as possible, and then get about the business of fulfilling it as only you can."

Oprah

CHAPTER 2

HOW TO START A NEW CHAPTER IN YOUR LIFE

There is something that I already know about you (even though you may not be aware of it).

You are unique, precious and one of a kind. For example, think about the probability of you even existing:

1) *Your parents had to meet, they had to have sex and your dad's sperm had to find your mum's egg (I know, too much information!)*

2) *Go further back – both sets of grandparents needed to meet.*

3) *Both sets of great grandparents had to meet theirs & theirs & so on.*

4) *The % chance of you being alive is so small.*

5) *The chance that you would be reading this book right now is even lower.*

I believe that YOU, yes, YOU are here for a reason – a very special reason.

The ups and downs of life can however, certainly take their toll on you, and you may ask yourself, "why am I here?" or, "is this all there is to life?"

Let me ask you, "Why do you get out of bed in the morning?"

Now you may say to earn money, or possibly to get the kids ready. Perhaps for you it's more functional, like to have a wee, or maybe you stay in bed till the afternoon?

However you've answered the above, my guess is that it's probably not really about WHY you get out of bed... these are just the things you do, right? But do you know WHY you do them? If this sounds like a difficult question to answer, or maybe even a trick question, don't worry. You're not alone. Just like you, most people don't know what their WHY is or how to find it.

In the following chapters of this book I'll show you how to choose a life of freedom, to live as the real you – authentic, satisfied, fulfilled and knowing why you are here. Knowing your function, as Oprah says. By reading this book, you'll begin to discover exactly what your purpose is as a living being, and how to live your life on your terms and no one else's. It all starts with finding your WHY!

Ok, so you may be thinking, "Cheryl, what do you mean by my WHY?" Allow me to explain...

Your WHY is your purpose, your calling, or you might even say your destiny. It's what inspires and drives you. It is the most important thing in your life, it's what you would fight day and night for, and it should be the motivation behind everything that you do. Unfortunately, so far, there is a good chance that you and many others have lived your lives without even knowing that you should have a WHY. As a result of not having your own WHY, maybe your life is dedicated to someone else's, making someone else's dream come true or helping someone else to achieve their goals.

Well, now it's time to focus on YOU!

This book is designed to help you Find Your WHY. Smile if that sounds like a good idea ☺

Why do you need to find your WHY?

Once you have found your own personal WHY, the world begins to make more sense. You must find it because it is what drives you, gives you energy and pulls your goals towards you. When you find it, it explains everything you do. It effects how you see the world, how you experience it, how you fit in and most importantly of all – it will prove to you that you really are wired for success.

So, you might be thinking, what do I mean 'wired' for success? By this I mean that the wiring in your brain, and in your nervous system, may need to be re-wired to help you if you want to make changes in your life.

STOP! Don't worry, there is no surgery required here (well not the hospital type, anyway!)

Let me explain. There is a feeling part of your brain, called the limbic system, and it knows when something feels right or wrong. Maybe you can remember a time when you just knew that something felt right or wrong?

When you find something that just feels right – it will encourage you, and it will give you energy and motivation. It helps you to work in harmony with your brain and your body, and that is why knowing your WHY is crucial for you.

To live without knowing your WHY could mean that you will just exist from day to day, like a fallen leaf from a tree being pushed by an external force, without any control.

Once you have found your WHY, you will know clearly why you do what you do, why you think how you think, why you make the choices you make and why you believe what you believe. Knowing your WHY makes decisions easy to make, because you can base your choices on a simple question – does this fit with my WHY or not?

So, is there a reason that women often follow someone else's WHY instead of their own? Let's take a look at our past to find out.

WOMEN IN SOCIETY

The role that women play in society has changed.

Let's go back to prehistoric times, where the role of a woman was purely as a procreator and a homemaker, to nurture and raise her offspring.

In more recent times, there was the industrial age, and during wartime British women worked in dirty and dangerous factory conditions, while the men went off to fight. Although women still earned much less than men, the increase in employability meant that families became more dependent on the wages of the wife, instead of just the husband.

It was just 100 years ago that Emmeline Pankhurst and the Suffragettes had their historical victory, winning the right for British women to vote. Can you even imagine living in those times, when women were seen as second-class citizens with no rights to own anything?

Even now, with more equality for women, there are still reminders of how women were previously regarded in society. For example, a single man is referred to as a Bachelor (sounds quite dashing right?) in contrast to the damming equivalent for a woman – Spinster.

Since the time of emancipation, the role of women has continued to change. One of the biggest shifts came with the birth control pill. Once contraception became widely available, women suddenly had a choice about procreation. To be a non-child bearing, single woman, was now a choice – and not just down to 'being left on the proverbial shelf'.

Living as a woman in a so-called 'man's world' has therefore become easier. Today, with all of the technology around us, we have so many choices and opportunities in many different walks of life. In particular as entrepreneurs or self-employed women, where the glass ceilings that keep women out of corporate boardrooms don't exist. According to The Office for National Statistics, in 2014 women made up just under one third of the self-employed (1.4 million). Since 2009, the number of self-employed women has increased by 34%. My belief is that this is not because women are looking to be equal with men in this area (the figures show that women are still well behind on overall figures), but because businesswomen bring nurturing and emotional elements to the male dominated boardroom, that are generally missing otherwise.

Here's a thought though. Is it really companies that create the glass ceilings, or is it that a woman's WHY is different from a man's?

The difference between a woman's WHY, and a man's WHY.

Men and women are the poles of humanity – yin and yang. While masculinity is stereotypically expressive, and femininity receptive – they are different and both powerful in their own right.

Are you an AA, an AAA or DD?

Like the positive and negative poles of a battery, both are needed to allow the energy to flow. From one pole the energy flows out, and from the other it flows in. Without both of them the battery would be dead. Humanity is the same. Without the yang of the masculine expressive outwardly focused energy, AND the yin of the feminine receptive inward focused energy, there would be no humanity!

Simply put, a man's WHY generally is about being an individual, standing out, competing, fighting and taking control.

In contrast, a woman is more than often about community, being part of a whole, being somebody significant through collaboration, co-operation and helping your own group, community, society or family. You help everyone around you become the best that they can be – you are more supportive and less competitive. However, sometimes these traits can also lead to women shrinking down and taking only supportive roles. Of course whilst this is a trait, I am not saying that it is black and white. There are some men that care for the community, just as there are some women who care about being an individual and taking control.

"Our deepest fear is not that we are inadequate. Our deepest fear is that we are powerful beyond measure. It is our light, not our darkness that most frightens us. We ask ourselves, who am I to be brilliant, gorgeous, talented, fabulous? Actually, who are you not to be? You are a child of God. Your playing small does not serve the world. There is nothing enlightened about shrinking so that other people won't feel insecure around you. We are all meant to shine, as children do. We were born to make manifest the glory of God that is within us. It's not just in some of us; it's in everyone. And as we let our own light shine, we unconsciously give other people permission to do the same. As we are liberated from our own fear, our presence automatically liberates others."

~ Marianne Williamson

Which leads me to ask the following questions:

"What is a woman's WHY?"

"What are you supposed to DO with your life?"

"What are you HERE for?"

What is a Womanly WHY?

If you were a woman in the 80s like me, you'll remember that we tried to make ourselves bigger. Using big hair, with Incredible Hulk sized shoulder pads, the aim was to make ourselves stand out. Even though fashion was becoming more feminine, women seemed hell bent on becoming more masculine. Phrases such as, "you can't be a successful career woman in a man's world without taking on the characteristics of a man" were thrown around with reckless abandon. In other words, you can't compete with men unless you act like a man. It's true that many of us turned into the men we wanted to marry!

However, as women we are NOT men, just as cats are not dogs (despite the O2 phone adverts). Women can only find real power if they become who they are, which is of course – a woman. That is why I wanted to write this book. I wanted to serve women, who are so commonly referred to as the opposite sex. Remember, opposite does not mean the same. We are different, and we have a voice!

Most of the literature, coaching, books, articles and blogs associated with using your WHY are based around a business WHY, and not a personal one. As we know, business is still dominated by men, so this means that current support is heavily weighted towards masculine traits. The reason for writing this book is because I want to focus on YOU and YOUR traits as a woman.

I'm a woman, too, and I love being a woman, but more importantly I love being a woman with a WHY. By helping YOU to find your WHY, then it will all be worth it.

"If just one woman says because of you I didn't give up, I know that my WHY has been achieved."

Cheryl Chapman

"IT IS IMPOSSIBLE TO LIVE WITHOUT FAILING AT SOMETHING, UNLESS YOU LIVE SO CAUTIOUSLY THAT YOU MIGHT AS WELL NOT HAVE LIVED AT ALL – IN WHICH CASE YOU FAIL BY DEFAULT."

- J.K.ROWLING

 Straight from the heart

Knowing your WHY helps you to decide want is right for you.

Be you. You're good enough.

Trust your intuition.

Do what makes you smile.

CHAPTER 3

HOW DO YOU ACT?

Find out with this quick quiz - I mean every girl loves a quiz – right?

1. How do you feel when you wake up on a Monday morning?

a)   *I know I have to get up because I can't let others down.*

b)   *I hit the snooze button and wish it was Saturday again.*

c)   *I feel energised, ready to live life to the full.*

d)   *I drag myself into the kitchen, drink my first energy drink and make a strong cup of coffee.*

2. After sharing a great idea with your friend, she tells you she thinks it's a bad idea. What's your reaction?

a)   *She's probably right, who do I think I am?*

b)   *I wish I never told her. Now I feel like a fool!*

c)   *I really don't care what she thinks, I know this is going to be a success.*

d)   *I decide to go to the pub and have a drink.*

3. A relationship that you thought was going somewhere special has ended, what are your thoughts?

a)   *I guess I wasn't the right person for them.*

b)   *Why does this always happen to me?*

c)   *As one door closes, another door opens.*

d)   *I must call the girls so I can go for a good night out.*

4. What is the number 1 thought that you have in any given day?

a)   *How can I make others happy?*

b)   *God I'm bored.*

c) *I am so happy and grateful for the life I have.*

d) *What can I eat/drink now?*

5. How would you describe your current situation?

a) *I am constantly busy helping others.*

b) *I feel trapped and unhappy.*

c) *I am living life to the full.*

d) *I am so busy that I have no time for myself.*

6. Where do you see yourself in five years' time?

a) *Wherever the special person in my life is.*

b) *Probably the same place I am now.*

c) *Exactly where my five-year plan is taking me.*

d) *I don't have time to plan.*

7. What do you think about change?

a) *It scares me. You don't know what might happen!*

b) *I can't see anything changing in my life.*

c) *It's what helps me to develop.*

d) *It's frustrating.*

8. Why do you think you're here?

a) *To make others happy.*

b) *To suffer sadness.*

c) *To be happy.*

d) *I don't know where I am.*

Results:

Please add up all your letter scores (A, B, C or D) and then insert your number score in the table below:

A	B	C	D

Mainly A-

You play the role of a people pleaser:

"I'm just a girl who can't say no?"

You tend to put other people's needs before your own.

Potentially, you could be relying on other people's opinions to make decisions in your life.

Concentrating on other people's problems is a way to avoid your own. You are avoiding the pain of being rejected and powerless, when you need to remind yourself that your worth is really much more than what you can ever do for others.

The good news: This book will show you a way to take back your power. By the end of the book you will no longer have to worry about pleasing other people, and you will realise the power of putting yourself before other people. Once you learn to say "NO", things will change for the better and people will have more respect for you; trust me!

Mainly B-

You play the role of a victim.

You tend to think that bad things only happen to you.

Potentially you could be attracting more negativity in your life.

You may be afraid of your own anger, denying it exists, projecting it onto others or waiting for aggression or harm from them. You are highly sensitivity to anger in others, and may even imagine that others have malicious intentions. Your anger is transformed into fear and distrust of others, and into feelings of being hurt or wounded.

The good news: Within this book you will learn how to take back control of yourself, your life and your emotions. By the end of the book you will know how to reconnect to your own feelings, accept them and express them safely. This alone will transform your life and you will realise the power of being your authentic self. Once you learn that you are in charge of your life, you'll never feel like a victim again! Hallelujah

Mainly C-

You play the role of positivity.

You look at the world in a positive light. Potentially, your glass is always half full, but what if your glass gets smashed? If you feel like you have to force yourself to see the positive things in every situation, then you're not allowing yourself to be complete and true to who you are. All emotions are valid. Whether we talk about them or not, they still happen.

The good news: Within this book I will show you how you can use your positivity in a way that will serve you, without eliminating the signs of possible danger. By the end of the book you will have clarity around your life, and find peace in knowing that sometimes you need the lows to appreciate the highs. Once you learn how to accept this, you will be able to live a life full of all emotions. Oh yeah!

Mainly D-

You play the role of the distractor.

You want to keep busy all the time.

You are not aware of how you are really feeling, because you use distracting techniques to keep you busy. This means that you don't have to access your true unresolved emotions. Learning how to resolve those emotions will free you from them, and allow you to focus on what you want rather than avoiding what you don't want.

The good news: Within this book you will learn how to take some time out from distraction. By the end of the book you will be able to appreciate the need for down time and the power of staying focused on one task at a time. Once you learn how to stop your mind from thinking so much, you will be able to complete tasks, and feel great whilst doing so!

So now that you have an idea of where you are starting from, let's begin a new chapter in your life. I am going to help you to improve the areas that are not currently serving you, or maybe even holding you back...

CHAPTER 4

TAKE A.I.M

So you might be thinking, "OK Cheryl. So I now know that according to your quiz, I'm a people pleaser. I'm a victim, I'm a positive Polly or even a distractor – so what?"

Well, you might be pleased to hear that you are not your behaviour. That's right, YOU are YOU, and your behaviour is something separate altogether. So why is this important? Well it means that you're not a victim or any of the above, even if your behaviour is. Which means that if you make a mistake, it does not make YOU a mistake, does that make sense? In other words you can make a mistake and it doesn't have to affect you or your life – you can learn from it.

For many years I felt trapped in my life, just thinking, "I guess this is my life, I better get on with it." Then as I started to open my mind to new people, new information and new possibilities, my life changed! After I decided to leave the corporate world, I chose a new direction, where I could use my people skills. I trained as a Life Coach and studied Neuro-Linguistic Programming and I was surprised to find that there were many women who had the same limiting beliefs that I had experienced. Many of the women I worked with had little or no sense of purpose. By working with my clients, I was able to help them to identify and overcome these limiting beliefs. I was able to help them create new stories for their future, and to help them find their WHY!

In order to 'Find Your WHY!' there are just 3 areas that you need to master:

Firstly, you need to have **AWARENESS**. This means that you need to know where you are right now, to understand what obstacles are currently blocking you from getting to where you would like to go. It is only once you remove the blocks that you can start to focus on your WHY. Just like a sat nav in a car, it's essential that you can tell your system where to start from. If not, you're not going to get particularly good directions. You need both a starting point, and a final destination/goal.

The 1st step of AWARENESS is to know where you are.

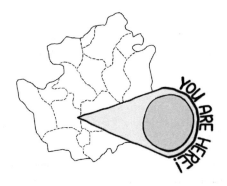

Where is your B?

Isn't it interesting that so many people have an opinion on what you should or shouldn't do with your life, and yet those people very rarely appear to have a perfect life themselves? If they spent more time on themselves, they might make some changes that would help them to live a life of freedom too.

The 2nd step of AWARENESS is knowing where YOU want to go.

Self-Belief

Have you ever had a time where you decided that you wanted to make a change in your life, only to hear a voice in your head saying, "you can't do that"? This is known as the voice of doom, doubt or dismissal. You need to have an awareness of these situations and more importantly, know what to do in order to turn the negativity around.

The 3rd step of AWARENESS is knowing how to believe in yourself!

Having AWARENESS is a great starting point in clearing out old beliefs to leave space for your WHY, but it isn't everything. You also need to know how to set the right INTENTION.

Intention is all about matching your WHY with your goals and ambitions. If you know where you are with awareness, then INTENTION is where you want to go and how you will enjoy the journey, as well as the eventual destination.

The key here is to be open to as many routes as possible, to get you to your place of happiness.

Life is all about setting INTENTION, it is just that sometimes we are not aware of what we are doing. Life isn't a wishing well. You cannot throw a coin in and expect a fairy to deliver your wishes. In reality, life is more like a mirror, which throws back whatever you put in front of it.

Mirror Mirror

If you put out a positive INTENTION, then it will show you a positive situation. Likewise, if you put out a negative one, it will show the same negativity back.

It's a bit like waking up in the morning in a really bad mood, where you expect the day to be a bad one. Then, that's exactly the sort of day you get. Have you ever heard the saying, "oh you look like you got out of the wrong side of the bed"? This is because I believe it's difficult for us to hide emotions, would you agree?

So, start to think about what you really want from life. What do you want to feel like every day, how do you want to be remembered, what do you want to do, who do you want to serve?

Key number 2 - You reap what you sow!

Finally, you have to learn how to **MANIFEST**. So you might be thinking, what on Earth is MANIFEST?

Well MANIFEST is all about putting something beyond doubt or question. It is about making it into a reality.

<u>Book it</u>

It's a bit like when you decide to go on holiday. Can you remember the last time when you wanted to get away from it all? Firstly, you decided where you wanted to go, how long you wanted to go for and who with, and then you took steps to make it happen. That's right, you helped to MANIFEST your holiday.

You may have heard of the concept of vision boards. Personally, I think this approach is fundamentally flawed. I can guarantee that most people who have one will have a fairly indifferent feeling towards it, and in most cases will not have achieved the life they dream of. To be able to truly MANIFEST, you not only need to use what you can see, but you must also be able to feel your way to the future.

If there was no failure in life, what would you do?

When you know how to MANIFEST, you can start to bring your WHY alive.

If you can see it in your mind, you can feel it in your hand!

The A.I.M is Happiness

What I teach my clients with The A.I.M is Happiness Programme for

AWARENESS is **The Conscious Realisation Strategy** ™

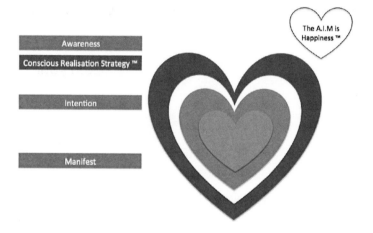

Here they learn how to be conscious about recognising where they are, who they are and what is holding them back. When you learn about these areas you will be able to understand what has happened to you in the past, helping you to shape your future.

My clients learn to share past experiences that can be unravelled with a simple and highly effective process. Experiencing this process allows you to find a positive in every situation.

As the saying goes, every cloud has a silver lining. Accepting that everything happens for a reason, and that life is about winning or learning, allows you to re-write the past and move forward.

With a strategy for turning a potential negative situation into a positive one, you are able to move forward and become the best version of you – right here, right now. Once you are able to consciously realise that you have all the tools you need, you will be able to focus on finding your WHY, to help you to focus on your future.

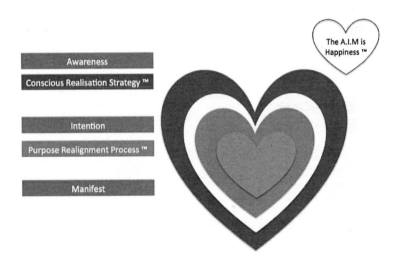

To help my clients set the right INTENTION, I use my **Purpose Realignment Process** ™

Here I teach my clients how to set goals, and I show them how they can be open to accepting that the end result will not always arrive by the route they expect. When you are able to master this element, you too will be able to attract what is in alignment with your WHY.

You will learn how success will help you to feel that you are living a life of true purpose.

My clients tell me that the feeling they have after this process is one of clarity, with a clear crystal 'knowing' that all is going to be well. When you know how to use your WHY to create a life of purpose, you too will be able to feel that sense of quiet reassurance, as you look to a clearer future.

With my **Dynamic Destiny Directive**™ my ladies see exactly how to MANIFEST into existence the life that they want, that will serve their WHY.

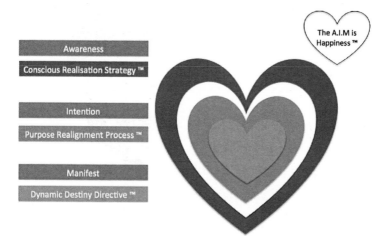

I would love to teach you how to take the everyday vision board and turn it into a sensational experience, one that will light you up every day as you bring your ideas into reality. When you use your WHY to look to the future, it is as if you are painting a picture of what is already happening right in front of you.

When you understand how to use these tools, you too will be able to take A.I.M and create the happiness you desire.

I would love to help you to start your journey, as this is something you should investigate further. In fact you **must** investigate further if you want to choose a life of freedom, and Find your WHY!

 Straight from the heart

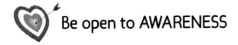 Be open to AWARENESS

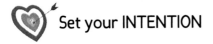 Set your INTENTION

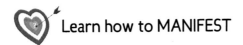 Learn how to MANIFEST

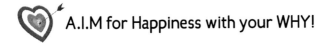 A.I.M for Happiness with your WHY!

"The history of all times and of today especially, teaches that women will be forgotten if they forget to think about themselves."

Louise Otto

CHAPTER 5

ON YOUR MARKS

To begin any journey, you must know where you are right now.

So what does that really mean?

It's important to take stock of where you are now, so that you can begin your journey towards realising your WHY. Let me ask you, when was the last time you took some time out, just for you?

Maybe you are a daughter, mother, grandmother, sister, friend, partner, or possibly you are all of these, and just to clarify these are just the potential roles you have in your private life, let alone your business! So if your answer is "I can't remember" or "it's been a while" then it's no surprise. When you couple this with your built in female tendencies of caring, sharing and building communities; traditionally you may believe that there is little or no time for you. Does that make sense?

The great news is that now is the time to make a change, and to put yourself first. Ask yourself the question, how can you continue to serve and help others if you are not in the right place yourself? A very good example of this is when you go on a holiday flight.

The air hostess will tell you, "In the case of loss of air pressure, oxygen masks will fall from above – please ensure you put the mask on yourself first, before attending to the needs of others." The same goes for your life. How many people can you look after if you're tired, ill, depressed or at worst dead? The answer is none. With that in mind, would you agree that now is the time to focus on you and to have an AWARENESS of where you are? I think you know the answer.

Let me start by clarifying what I mean by AWARENESS. The dictionary defines AWARENESS as having knowledge and consciousness, which means you are able to listen to yourself, recognise how you feel and pay attention to YOU.

In order for YOU to be able to realise your WHY, for YOU to improve YOUR life and for YOU to have more happiness, you need to have Self-Awareness. It's all about you!

Who Am I?

OK I get it Cheryl, sounds easy, but where do I start?

Most people identify themselves by their position in society, their job or their role. However, this is not who YOU are. These are the things you do and the roles that you play. You shouldn't allow the needs and desires of your body, and the emotional and intellectual expressions of your mind, to define your identity. For example, "I'm not very clever and I'm out of shape" or, "I'm just a bag of nerves and I'm never going to amount to anything".

I'm here to tell you that there is a much better way to contemplate the real nature of your existence and it starts with asking yourself a different question: "Who am I?"

The importance of awareness is about learning how to understand why you feel what you feel and why you behave the way you do. Once you begin to understand this concept, you'll have the opportunity and freedom to change things about yourself.

You may not remember the first time you looked in a mirror and saw your own reflection, however, I am sure you have seen children do this. Their reaction is amazing – a mixture of curiosity, wonder and joy. This is the same as when you remind yourself as an adult that you ARE an individual, that you remember you are you and that you are here for a reason. That reason is to live a life of discovery, just like when you were a child.

Once you can see yourself and where you are, you can then begin to get more aligned with your WHY. In turn, this means that you can create the life that you want.

It's impossible to change and become self-accepting if you are not willing to hold a mirror up to your life, does that make sense?

In this chapter I want you to review your current life, reflect and focus on developing awareness. By working with thousands of people all around the world, I have found that there are 8 key areas of your life that you must be fully aware of in order to take control of your own destiny.

By identifying and prioritising these aspects of your life, you will be able to focus on and improve them. This means that you can become aware of how things are for you, what areas you are happy with and what still needs to change in order for you to feel more fulfilled. Then, you can move in the direction that you want to go.

The key, of course, to have balance across all aspects of your life, otherwise it would be like driving a car with one or two wonky wheels!

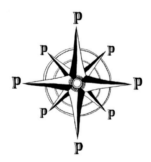

Compass Clarification Process™.

My Compass Clarification Process™ can help you to review these 8 areas. So grab yourself a pen and a piece of paper and start to make notes about how happy you are in the following areas:

1. Profession

Are you doing what you love to do? Can you bring love to what you do? Does it support your heart's desire and support others?

2. Partner

Do you have a great relationship? Do you look forward to their company? Do you smile when you think of them?

If you're single, are you mingling, having fun and enlightening those you meet?

3. People

Do you have close positive friendships with others who cheer you on? Are you adding new friends and colleagues regularly? Are you expanding on the kinds of people you meet, in order to expand yourself?

Do you look forward to being with your family or are you holding grudges still? Do you let them be themselves, with no need to change? No one has a perfect family. They don't need to change. We need to change ourselves. They help us practice unconditional love.

4. Physiology

What is your health & fitness like? Do you eat energising food, take regular exercise and relax? How do you treat your body?

5. Play

Are you playing? Really playing? Do you laugh a lot, be silly, and take out your inner child at least once a week? Do you take action to overcome fears (like skydiving)?

Do you take time for leisure either on your own or with your partner/family?

6. Physical environment

What does your car, home, workspace and wardrobe look like in terms of organization?

7. Personal Development

Are you learning, reading and expanding who you are? Are you exercising your mind?

How do you connect to your inner world? Do you experience inner peace and a sense of connection with others?

8. Prosperity

Are you are living a lifestyle you love? Do you feel rich from a financial point of view, as well as an emotional point of view?

Once you have made your notes on each of these areas, take the following 3 simple steps:

Score - I ask my clients at my 'Live, Love, Laugh Workshop' to give each of the 8 areas a score out of 10 (10 is fab, down to 1 representing an area that you are not happy with)

Sequence - Now rank the above points in terms of score

Solve - This is the area where you use processes and techniques to help you correct your course.

I show my clients how to bring balance into their lives. When you are able to do this, you will be able to go to where you want to be. This leads to realignments for you and your WHY.

As you begin to realign with your WHY, you will score higher on all these aspects, and consequently you will find that you improve your relationships, career, wealth, health and happiness.

Throughout this process you will discover new things about yourself, and new truths that will expand your awareness. Think of awareness as a circle. Everything inside and outside the circle is yourself, but you are only able to see and know what is inside the circle.

As you expand your circle of awareness, you will get to know much more about yourself. You'll learn what you are capable of, you'll learn your true potential and you'll learn about the incredible possibilities that the future holds. The more doors you open, the more doors you will discover are still yet are to be opened. AWARENESS is the very beginning of your personal development.

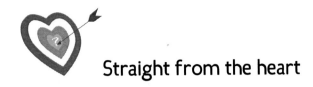 Straight from the heart

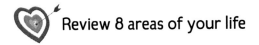 Review 8 areas of your life

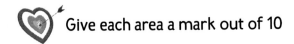 Give each area a mark out of 10

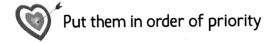 Put them in order of priority

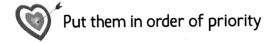 Take action to address these areas

"Every day, think as you wake up: Today I am fortunate to have woken up. I am alive. I have a precious human life. I am not going to waste it.

The Dalai Lama

CHAPTER 6

GET SET

Now that you have awareness of who you are, where you are and what blocks need to be removed, you can change from a 'I don't want this' mind-set – to one that can bring you more of what you do want. It is now time to understand how to develop clarity of mind.

Without this next crucial element, you may wander around accepting whatever life sends you and perhaps you will never be in a position to use your WHY to its full potential ☺

So, what am I talking about? Allow me to explain:

In order to identify and realise your goals, you need to know how to set the correct INTENTION.

So you might be thinking, what is intention?

Maybe like me, you have heard about an intention with regards to a man's intention to marry a woman (ok so maybe I read too many Rom Com books!) so an intention is a plan of action.

Intention without action is useless, and the same can be said about setting goals. Goals and intentions are equally important, but are also fundamentally different from one another.

The difference between a goal and an INTENTION

Intention is based on your inner world, your feelings, your passion, your values, your purpose and your WHY.

While goals are external, they are the things, situations or places that will bring the desired inner experience.

For example, let's look at the very well know SMART goal setting process (commonly attributed to Peter Drucker).

SMART is an acronym for:

Specific

Measurable

Assignable

Realistic

Timed

So a goal using this set of criteria could be, "I will make £100,000 by the 31st December 2015. I will achieve this by hitting all of the monthly sales target set by my manager."

Would you agree this goal is specific? In terms of monetary value, the answer is yes. It provides clear and measurable targets to hit, the task is assigned to the person setting the goal and relies on the manager setting the targets, it also appears realistic and it is timed for completion by the end of the year. All in all, the five elements of SMART goal setting are used, so it's a good goal, right?

A goal is usually one thing at one point in time. It's very black and white, without any grey area. It's a bit like a game of football – you either score a goal or you don't – there are no ½ points for effort! In other words you either achieve your goal, or you don't!

The problem with goals is that, while moving you towards what you want, they can take you out of the moment and create a feeling that what you have isn't enough, that you haven't quite made it yet, or that you are not enough!

Ask yourself the following question: If your goal is to get from A to B, and the only route you will consider is a straight line, what happens if there is a block along the way? How do you get there? Do you just return to point A feeling like a failure?

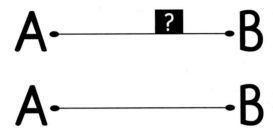

When you use intention, you remove the black and white nature of thinking from your mind. You start approaching 50 shades of grey, and I'm sure you know how much more interesting that can be ☺

The reason for this is that intention is not governed by the details of a goal. In other words, when you set the intention, you are allowing for the energy of the Universe to deliver you what you are looking for – in the way that it sees fit.

Now you might be thinking, "HANG ON Cheryl! The Universe delivers? Is this some new parcel delivery service, like UPS or DPD?!" If this is new to you, it might take quite a leap of faith to accept that statement. To be honest, the first time I heard this as a suggestion, my first thought was, "What a load of rubbish!"

Let's review this by going back to the original goal:

"I will make £100,000 by the 31st December 2015. I will achieve this by hitting all of the monthly sales targets set by my manager."

Let's imagine for a minute that you have set this goal. You know that you can't just sit cross legged and pray for your targets to hit themselves, and therefore you know that you have to take action. However, by being so specific about how this money will come to you and what you need to do to achieve it, would you agree that you have to be laser focused?

Let's consider what could happen if you had 'blinkers on'. In other words, you are blind to the other opportunities that could be around you:

> *You don't buy a winning lottery ticket?*

> *You are so busy that you don't go and visit an elderly relative that forgets about you in their will?*

> *You don't attend an event where a person was looking to work with someone like you, and wanted to pay a retainer up front?*

Now I'm not saying that 'what ifs' are a way to live your life, my point is that when you set a goal so specifically, it leads you to thinking that it can only be achieved in one way. In turn, this leads to you deleting or dismissing other opportunities, that the Universe brought your way.

It is a little bit like looking for the man of your dreams. You could be so focused on a tall, dark and handsome man that you miss out on your soul mate, all because you were focused on looks.

In other words, you can still set a goal as long as you incorporate an intention. Just make sure that you include emotions, your values and that your goal is in line with your WHY. Once you've done all that, then you have to be open for the Universe to deliver you some alternative ways to achieve what you want.

Let's take another look at the previous goal, and turn it into an intention:

"I will make £100,000 by the end of this year. I will do this by doing what I love, having fun, helping others to achieve what they want and making a difference in the world."

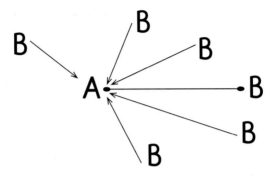

As you can see, intention is the energy behind the goal. It's your desire, your WHY, the power that gives meaning not only to the goal, but also to the experience you have in the process.

Without intention, goals are binary. In other words, they simply require a straightforward yes or no. With intention, you have a motive and a purpose. You open opportunities for future success.

Goal setting is a valuable skill that helps us to stay on track, whilst intention gives us the 'fuel' to get things done. Without goals, you'll have no direction, no destination and ultimately no achievement. Therefore, they are both essential for completing tasks and getting what you want.

A goal is a what, and intention includes the how and the WHY.

Things to consider when planning your INTENTION

The problem is that most people don't know what they want.

Ask them what they what and generally they will give you a long list of – "well I don't want this and I don't want that."

Do you know anyone like that?

What this means is that most of the people you meet will never reach their full potential. They are too busy focusing on what they don't want instead of putting the energy into what they do want. It is a bit like trying to lose weight. Now, I have to tell you, I have tried just about every technique in the book for this. Whether it's counting calories, eating just protein, different coloured days, stuffing my face with eggs (not pleasant for anyone in a 2 mile radius!!), not eating after 8pm, juicing vegetables, eating natural foods only – the list goes on. However, whenever I tried to lose weight I was only focusing on what I couldn't eat. The inevitable result of this was that ALL the foods I couldn't eat – like chocolate – suddenly became the only food that I could think about.

Maybe you have had a similar experience?

My most successful weight loss came when I was focused on what I wanted, for example to be healthier, so I could be fitter for travelling around the world to connect with large audiences.

I believe it all starts with setting the right intention.

As you can see, success came on the occasions when my intention was set for a higher purpose, one that was aligned with my WHY. By higher purpose, I mean a purpose where you are not limiting yourself to certain outcomes or procedures. In other words, I stopped focusing on the goal. I started to trust that aligning my values, principles and enjoying the experience, would achieve the goal.

In order to have all of this, you need to be able to set a clear intention. When the intention is right, any goal will be achievable.

You might be thinking, "OK Cheryl, this all sounds like it's too good to be true. How does it work?" The answer is simple. By setting powerful intentions, you're BOUND to succeed in realising your goals, because it means that you'll live your life with a purpose. Purpose is what you want to do, and how and WHY you want to do it.

I am sure, like me, that you have dreams, ambitions, goals or aspirations. Things that you want to do or become. But sometimes life gets in the way of those dreams, doesn't it?

It reminds me of when I first started to attend the Professional Speaker Academy. Andy – the founder, was asking for volunteers to help him at his events. I remember Andy was on stage and if you'd been there with me you would have been sitting at the back of the room watching him talking to the audience:

"When you are building a business you must be able to systemise it, stop making it about you the personality and allow it to be taught to others."

Ping! Have you ever had a 'light bulb moment?'

"Hey, I could learn from this. Andy is going to need some help, he doesn't have anyone to deliver his content – it's going to be me!" That was the day my intention was set ☺

Now I didn't know how, when or where this was going to happen, I just knew WHY! There were no **Specifics**, nothing **Measureable** (other than that I knew I had to learn his content), nothing **Assigned** (Andy didn't even know I had decided this) and it wasn't **Realistic** either. I had never spoken on a large stage, or coached anyone. Nor did I set a date, so nothing was **Timed**. What I did set, was my INTENTION. I just knew that one day I would be on stage delivering his content. I felt as if it had already been achieved.

So, I started to take action. I learned his content, ensured I was around him as much as possible, and then one day – sitting outside the office on a beautiful summer afternoon – I heard the words that I'd been waiting for:

"Cheryl, you have been giving a lot to my company and I'd like to offer you the opportunity to deliver some content at the next event in Johannesburg – are you interested?"

Bingo! This is exactly what I was waiting to hear. My intention and hard work had generated a positive opportunity for me, and there was no way I was going to turn this down! However, I didn't want to say yes straight away! After all, a girl has to play it cool, right?

"Thanks Andy, I'll check my diary and get back to you when I get home tomorrow."

So, fast forward 5 weeks and you find me standing in front of a 200 plus audience in Johannesburg, delivering content, blowing them away…goal achieved, right?

However, 30 minutes later…

"Please welcome back to the stage – Mr. Andy Harrington"

My delivery should have been over 60 minutes. I froze. I couldn't remember my own name, let alone any content!

If you'd have been in the room that day, you'd have seen me with tears running down my face as I rushed to the exit, and waited for the taxi to take me to the airport.

Now, here's the thing. If this had been a goal, I would have succeeded. I had stood on stage and delivered Andy's content. The problem is that this wasn't just a goal. This was an INTENTION, and as such I was emotionally involved. My WHY was to serve the audience and Andy, and so as I sat crying in the taxi, I realised how badly I wanted this. I wanted to deliver Andy's content in a way that would inspire them to share their messages of hope and help. I could not leave this one box unticked.

I kept my intention alive. Slowly but surely, Andy gave me new opportunities, which led to other opportunities for me to speak and teach across the globe. At the time of writing I have just spoken at two women-only events. The first of these was 'Damsels in Success', where I shared a stage with Ali Brown. Ali was recently named Entrepreneurial Guru for Women, by Business News Daily, so this was quite an experience. The second event, 'Queens of Life', took place in Poland and was much bigger. I spoke to an audience that was around 2000 strong, and shared the stage with some of Poland's most influent female speakers; as well as Allan Pease, the Author of *Why Men Lie and Women Cry*.

Are you ready to set your INTENTION? Are you ready to receive the opportunities that life will show you? Or are you too blinkered to see them?

The good news is that it doesn't have to be this way. Learning how to use the power of intention means that you will know how to make life help you. You can do anything you choose to, and anything you intend to do can be used to achieve your goals.

Why are intentions important?

Intentions give you a framework for you to set priorities. They help you to use your time wisely, and to make sure that you have all the resources needed, in order to manifest your goals. Just by setting and then working towards your intentions, you will be declaring to the whole universe that you are serious about your dreams and goals.

A strong, positive, and energized intention will attract everything that is needed to make it happen.

Have you ever experienced a time when you really wanted something, but when it came, it didn't arrive from where you had expected it to? A good example is when you were a child, and wanted a certain gift. I remember one year my sister wanted an 'A La Carte Kitchen', and we hunted high and low for it.

"Oh, those are the must-have toy this year – we are all sold out!" was the regular response. As Christmas Eve approached, my Mum and Dad were at their wits end...then came the phone call:

"Hello, is that Mrs Brooks? Ah good, we'd like to congratulate you. You are the winner of our annual prize draw – you have won first prize!"

You guessed it, an 'A La Carte kitchen'!

Now here's the strange thing, none of us could even remember entering a draw. So maybe the Universe heard us calling?

I remember another time when I had very little money and I was desperate. The bills were mounting up, and more importantly I needed food to eat. Just when I felt like I was on my knees, I received a letter from the tax office. I remember opening the brown envelope with the HMRC stamp and wanting to be sick. I read the letter twice – a TAX REBATE! You cannot imagine the relief I felt that day.

So to sum up, intentions can be set for EVERYTHING you do. Before you start to set your own intentions, you should ask yourself the following questions:

What is my WHY?

What do I want to get out of this experience?

What is the result I'm looking for?

How will I feel when this is achieved?

What am I bringing to this experience?

Remember to set the intention, take action and be open to receive.

"Intentions are the breath of your goals, they are the wind beneath the wings of your dreams and only through intention can your goals fly. Intentions fill you with life, with energy and with love. They lift to you and remind you why you have your goals. Intentions gently nudge you, whisper to you and encourage you. Intentions help you connect to your truth and keep you aligned and in harmony. They help to balance the masculine energy of goals with the feminine energy of holding space so that those goals can be realise. Make your intentions ones that fits with your WHY!"

Anon

Straight from the heart

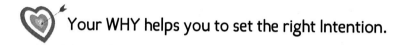 Your WHY helps you to set the right Intention.

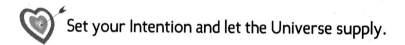 Set your Intention and let the Universe supply.

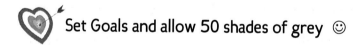 Set Goals and allow 50 shades of grey ☺

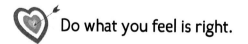 Do what you feel is right.

"Success is liking yourself, liking what you do and liking how you do it"

Maya Angelou

CHAPTER 7

GO!

Now you can start to create the life you want. Yes, that's right, YOU can create!

Ok, you might be thinking – here you go again Cheryl. Do you think I'm some sort of creator?

The answer is yes! Just as you have become aware of where you are, and that your goals need to be set with a strong intention, you are well on your way to attracting everything you want in your life. All you need to do, is MANIFEST. As you know, this doesn't mean that you have to take yourself off to an isolated range of mountains in the deepest darkest part of Peru, in search of some incredible witchcraft. Nor does it mean that you can just sit cross legged on your settee at home – surrounded by candles – chanting in the hopes that a million notes will land in your lap.

MANIFEST is by no means a new word. In fact it first appeared around 1350, and was used to describe something that was visible. I am using the word here in the context of being able to 'see' an image in your mind, and then bringing it into your life. This means that you won't only be able to 'see' it, but also to feel, smell, taste and touch it.

For over 25 years, vision boards have been almost universally perceived as the best means of manifesting. Vision boards are physical (a pin board for example) or a digital version that are filled with images of how you would like your life to look in the future. Creating a vision board is a very simple process, and this is one of the reasons that they are so popular.

So, you might be thinking, what do I do with the board?

Well, one school of thought is to have it with you all the time, in order to make sure you can see it every day, all day. This means that you are constantly being bombarded with the positive images, which serve as on going reminder of what you want. The other advice is to forget about it and let the Universe supply (the good old Universe again ☺)

I personally believe that the whole vision board concept is a waste of time for most people.

"What Cheryl? But hang on, didn't you say that I'm the creator?"

Yes, I did and don't get me wrong, there are many examples of vision board success. This includes:

Jim Carey

Considering giving up on his dream as a struggling comedian after he got booed off stage, Jim decided to pursue his passion. He decided to visualise his success by writing himself a cheque for $10 million, adding a note that read, "for acting services rendered". He told Oprah Winfrey that that his 1st film deal for Dumber & Dumber was for...you guessed it – $10 million!

Oprah Winfrey

Tells of how she helped someone else's vision come true, just by using a board.

On the morning of the presidential election – November 4, 2008 – Oprah called New York City radio station Power 105.1 and shared the following story:

"I was speaking with Michelle [Obama] and Caroline Kennedy and Maria Shriver – we were all doing a big rally out in California. At the end of the rally Michelle Obama said something powerful: "...I want you to leave here and envision Barack Obama taking the oath of office". I created a vision board. I had never had a vision board before. I came home, I got me a board and put Barack Obama's picture on it, and I put a picture of the dress I wanted to wear to the inauguration."

Lucinda Cross

As a young college student, she made a bad choice that landed her in prison. However, instead of becoming another sad statistic, she chose to learn from her mistake. She chose to take control of her life, and build a better future for herself.

Today she is an entrepreneur, bestselling author, speaker and life coach who's been featured on such prestigious media outlets as ABC, NBC, Black Enterprise, Essence Magazine and many more. She attributes all her success to vision boards and has literally built her business around them.

> "Whether you look at it from a spiritual or scientific aspect, this world is a huge vision board. Everything that's here is because it started as an image someone had in his or her mind. You want to call it a blueprint, or a business plan? Fine. But first, they had to think about it and draft it. So a vision board? It's like selling our own ideas to ourselves."

Lucinda Cross

Maybe you're thinking that I've lost the plot now, saying that I think these boards are a waste of time, but then proving that they work. Let me explain.

For the majority of people, a vision board is just a process that they go through. They collect 2D flat images from glossy magazines, with a selection process that is more akin to a child selecting Christmas gifts from the latest Argos catalogue. In other words, it is more than likely that their selection is based on quantity rather than quality. In turn, this could mean that the emotion attached to these images is about as strong as the emotion used when picking out which toilet roll to use!

With this in mind, 3 years ago I decided to find out how others viewed their vision boards. To do this, I conducted a survey. The results were quite startling.

The participants of my survey were a group of people who were all involved in personal development programmes. Before I tell you what questions I asked, if you have a board, STOP reading now! Go get it, look at it and answer the questions in the space provided:

1) *Why did you create your board?*

2) *When did you create this board & when was the last time you looked at your board/image?*

3) *Where do you keep your board/image?*

4) *Describe the condition of your board/image?*

5) *Describe your board (as if I was on the end of a telephone call, so I can make a picture of your board in my head)*

6) What do you feel about your board/image?

7) What changes would you make if you could?

Here are some of the more frequent comments that came back; maybe these are the same as some of yours?

1) Why did you create your board?

To attract wealth/so I could focus on my future/to realise my dream.

2) When did you create this board & when was the last time you looked at your board/image?

5 years ago/ 2 years ago/this year.

3) Where do you keep your board/image?

On my laptop/on my wall in my living room/office.

4) Describe the condition of your board/image?

Looks lived in/scruffy/it needs redoing.

5) Describe your board (as if I was on the end of a telephone call, so I can make a picture of your board in my head)

It has a lot of colour photos on it/it contains a lot of positive words & slogans/ it shows images of the life of my dreams/it shows pictures and words to describe the life I want.

6) What do you feel about your board/image & state why?

Sad – this reminds me of what I haven't yet achieved/it makes me feel overwhelmed/I don't feel anything.

7) What changes would you make if you could?

I think it all needs redoing/none – I will wait until this one materialises/ none I don't think it works.

The Common Denominator

Let me ask you a question with reference to the answers received. Do you think these were indicative of the people who had achieved a lot of success with vision boards or not? Let's take a look.

Write down what you have already achieved:

> *I visited some of the places on my board. I have done some of the activities on the board. I have a new car/I have achieved some of what is shown on the board, but there is so much more that I expected.*

That's correct – very little success, if any at all.

With these comments in mind, let's review why that could be:

There was no obvious connection between when the board was created, nor where it was kept. Nor was it to do with how many times it was viewed, what the condition of the board was, or even what was on the board itself. I believe the problem with the majority of vision boards is that they rely only on what you see!

Reviewing their answers to how they used the board made them feel sad, and I believe that this lack of enthusiasm is the key! Feeling sad, overwhelmed or even disinterested when looking at what should be your dream, is tantamount to saying, "Don't bother sending me anything good – I don't want it."

Think about this for a moment. If you found the partner of your dreams (maybe they are on your board) but acted like you weren't interested – do you think they would stick around? The answer is NO!

What about the car you've got on your board – have you ever driven it? From my survey, most people hadn't even sat in the car that they had on their board, let alone driven it. Similarly, it may look good to have a large detached mansion in the middle of nowhere, but if you don't like the feeling of isolation – it's not going to be for you, is it? Does that make sense?

How to change the outcome

You must start with your WHY!

What is it that excites you? What lights you up, and what do you really want to happen in your life?

With my **Dynamic Destiny Directive**™, I work with my clients to create sensation boards, so that all of the senses are activated. This means that not only will you like what you see, but you will create a total stimulation of emotions, in order to ensure that you will be inspired by your future.

All of this starts with knowing how to create the correct ambience and emotional state.

Using all of the senses allows you to tap into your very essence – so that you can see, hear, feel, touch, taste and even smell your dream. Your dream and your WHY are interconnected. Every time you even think about your dream, you will feel a connection with your WHY. This connection will pull and attract you towards it, like iron fillings to a magnet.

Finally, another crucial element is that you should ACT as IF you already have what is on your board. The reason for this is that the mind cannot separate what actually IS verses what is imagined. Now, I know you might be thinking, "Yeah ok, Cheryl, but I don't live in an 8 bedroom mansion by the sea. I don't drive a flash car, so how can I do that?"

Well, it all goes back to this – imagine how you would feel if you did?

That's right, you can still feel the pleasure of having what you want, and of being who you want to be. When you are living with a strong WHY, it is easy to know what that is.

Why? Because you just know that it is in alignment with you. You and your WHY are one and the same.

It's as if the doorbell is ringing with a bespoke express delivery, just for you.

 Straight from the heart

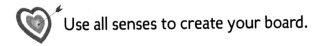 Use all senses to create your board.

 Ensure you are in the correct state before creating.

Know what you want by aligning with your WHY!

Live, Breathe & Feel it.

CHAPTER 8

THE TARGETTED APPROACH

So now you know that to have **AWARENESS**, to be able to set your **INTENTION** & then **MANIFEST** your life of freedom, there is a vital ingredient. This ingredient will help you to stay calm, in control and congruent to the life that is for you. The key ingredient is your WHY!

So, you might be thinking, "Cheryl that's great and all I've read here makes perfect sense, but how do I know if I know my **WHY**???"

In this chapter, I will ask you a number of questions, that will help you to **Find Your WHY**!

Before we begin the exercises, I need you to take some time away from any distractions. Find a quiet room in your house, a place outdoors or even in your car. Wherever your quiet place is, make sure that you are on your own. This process will take around 1 hour.

Have a glass of water nearby, as you need to stay hydrated.

Please be prepared to go deep, be vulnerable, be honest and go with whatever comes to you first.

You can complete these questions in this book, or on alternative pieces of paper. However, if you go to the website below, you will be able to complete the questions online. I will then be able to personally assess them for you and provide feedback:

www.getmywhy.com

Setting

Imagine that you found yourself as a contestant on a reality programme. You have a golden ticket, which means that you will be on the programme for the full year that it is running.

The place that you are going to live in will be with another 11 contestants. They can speak the same language as you, and you will have all the basics that you need; such as food, warmth and shelter. However, you will not have any access to technology. This means no telephones, no television and no computers (if you are old enough to remember back to the 70's!). There is a prize at the end of the show, but no one knows if it is a team prize or an individual one.

PART 1

Question 1

What do you do to pass your time, that serves you as an individual?

Question 2

What do you do to pass your time, that serves the team?

Question 3

What type of people would you hang about with?

Question 4

What type of people would you avoid?

PART 2

Imagine that you have been in the programme for 3 months. Suddenly, you are awoken in the middle of the night and told that there is a change in the rules. The prize is only going to be for 1 person.

Question 5

What do you do to pass your time, that serves you as an individual?

Question 6

What do you do to pass your time, that serves the team?

Question 7

What type of people would you hang about with?

Question 8

What type of people would you avoid?

PART 3

Imagine that you have been in the programme for 6 months. Suddenly you are awoken in the middle of the night and told that there is a change in the rules again. Now the prize is going to be for every person, but only if everyone in the group is regarded as part of the group.

Question 9

What do you do to pass your time, that serves you as an individual?

Question 10

What do you do to pass your time, that serves the team?

Question 11

What type of people would you hang about with?

Question 12

What type of people would you avoid?

PART 4

As part of the reality programme, there are many tasks that you have to take part in.

Please complete the following ones:

Imagine that you have been told that are going to die in 6 months' time and that you have to plan your own funeral.

Question 13

Choose a song to play at your funeral that would represent your life:

Question 14

Choose a headstone from the following images or draw your own:

Question 15

If you could only choose one word for your headstone, which describes how you would like to be remembered, what would that word be?

Question 16

In one sentence, how would you like to be remembered?

Question 17

Choose someone to read your eulogy:

a) *What relationship are they to you?*

b) *Why did you choose them?*

c) *What would they say about you?*

Question 18

Choose one person that you want to write a love letter to. This can be to anyone who is dead or alive:

a)   *What relationship are they to you?*

b)   *Why did you choose them?*

Question 19

Write the letter to them now.

PART 5

Imagine that you have been told that you have been given another 5 years to live

Question 20

Write yourself a bucket list (a list of 20 things you want to do before you die). For the purposes of this list, you should assume that money is no object.

1)

2)

3)

4)

5)

6)

7)

8)

9)

10)

11)

12)

13)

14)

15)

16)

17)

18)

19)

20)

Finally, if you haven't already done so, please transfer this information onto the online template here: **www.getmywhy.com**

Once you have submitted your answers to the questions, I will personally analyse your responses before sending you a copy of your WHY (in PDF format).

The benefit for you is that you will then get to understand what each of the questions you have answered represent. I will be able to help you to Find Your WHY, and in doing so will help you to make decisions for your life – based on YOUR purpose.

If someone asks you to do something, you can check if this is in keeping with your WHY. If it isn't, you can decline. Unlike in the past where you may have felt uncomfortable with doing this, you now know with certainty that this is the ONLY answer you should be giving.

You will now have a reason to get out of bed, and your future will be one that you can plan. In other words, you can set your sights and A.I.M for the life that you want. My A.I.M in writing this book is to help you to expand your AWARENESS, to increase your INTENTION and to encourage you to MANIFEST what you want into your life. This is because my WHY is to help other women like you. I want to be able to connect with your purpose, and to tap into your natural talents, which means that you will start to attract those who resonate with you, to be a part of this incredible journey called life.

Knowing my WHY has helped me to do this and connect with many like-minded women all over the world, who want to make a difference.

One of those women, who you have already heard of, was Marion. Marion has helped me to understand the limitations that I didn't even know I had. I thought you might be interested in hearing from the lady herself ....

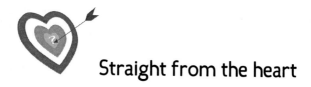

Straight from the heart

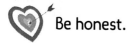 Be honest.

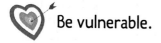 Be vulnerable.

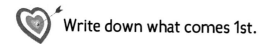 Write down what comes 1st.

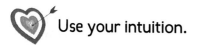 Use your intuition.

CHAPTER 9

MARION

Have you ever experienced a time when your life felt good? I mean really good, as if you'd made it?

It's 1998. I'm sitting at my desk in the IT department of Mercedes Benz Finance. Next to me is Chris. He's everything you'd imagine a typical 'computer geek' to be, with his black rimmed glasses and tank top over his shirt (what are tank tops actually for?). We are knee- deep in computer code, and I'm handing over the work I've just completed to him.

"So... umm... Marion, how come you're leaving? You've only been here for 6 months. I mean you are such a creative programmer and you're brilliant at what you do. If you took that job they've offered you, you'd be rolling in it!"

"Well Chris, the truth is, being an IT contractor is only a means to an end. I'm only working here to earn the money to fund my travels. 6 months' work means I've got enough for my next trip. My motto is – work to live, don't live to work! Life's not all about the money."

I can see the look of disbelief on his face – it's a look I see a lot.

I don't expect it to resonate with a guy in his twenties! My travels take me out of the corporate world, and into a world of fascination and new opportunities. It's a perfect mix, and I'm having the time of my life!

Little did I know what was about to happen. Something which completely changed the way I looked at the world.

You might be thinking, "WOW what did you do, find religion or a new way of life?"

Well, no it was actually something that literally changed the way I looked at the world.

"Dr... you know you prescribed me with those tablets to help with my thyroid problem? Well I've noticed that my eyes, especially the left eye, have begun to get bigger. It's like it is bulging from the socket, and because of this I keep getting double vision."

"Ah yes, Miss Bevington, this is one of the possible side effects. It does state this on the leaflet." (Note to self – read the leaflet!)

Now, have you ever heard of the saying, "For every cloud there is a silver lining"? I couldn't carry on with my IT work, as concentrating on a screen with double vision was not practical.

However, on my travels I had an amazing opportunity to help run some yoga classes. You might be thinking that sitting down on the floor cross-legged with your eyes closed is a great way to avoid double vision... EXACTLY!

It was during one of my Shavasana classes (a yoga technique that requires lying on your back) that I had another eye opener!

Barbara rushes in. 65 years old – she's a tall, blonde, ball of energy and has a look of Helen Mirren about her. I remember in her first class how difficult she found it, but she's improved leaps and bounds.

"Marion, I'm sorry I'm late, but I've got something to show you – I can't believe how amazing I feel. Look at my arm!"

As she speaks, she swings both her arms straight up, reaching for the ceiling, "Marion you're a miracle worker!" She hugs me tight as the other members of the class begin to gather around.

""Marion, I've had physiotherapy, so many different types of massage and even acupuncture, and I still haven't been able to do that for over 20 years!"

"Barbara, that is great news for you! OK everyone, settle down, and let's begin."

I can feel the tears beginning to fill my eyes, as a profound sense of pride, satisfaction, fulfillment and gratitude overwhelms me.

Have you ever had a time when you can hear a voice in your head? The voice is loud and clear, "This is what you should do!"

I was filled with a deep sense of knowing, like nothing I'd ever had before.

Now I know, looking back at the time, that this was the beginning of realising my WHY. I'd found what really satisfies me, which is helping myself and others to connect to our authentic essence, by using the body to help feed the mind and soul.

I can hear you saying, "What? All that, just by sitting cross-legged and lying on your back?!"

Well yes, that is one of the core parts of yoga, but what touched me on that day was the essence of yoga – it's so much bigger than the poses. I'm talking about a way of life. I spent the next 2 years in India living and breathing yoga. I trained to be a teacher and yoga therapist. However, I felt like there was more to discover and I knew I still needed to develop my understanding to help heal myself. Yes, I still saw 2 of everything, even opportunities ☺

Skip ahead to 2009, and I'm in the famous London Moorefield's Eye Hospital, looking around at white-washed medical walls. The room smells clinical.

"Miss Bevington, your condition has deteriorated severely. There's a chance that you could lose your vision, but the good news is we can help you..."

"You must be joking Doc, I've lived like a saint for the past 2 years! How can this be getting worse? Sorry Doctor, what has caused this?"

He looks a bit frustrated, "Well, as I just said, we don't know the cause. Your body is attacking itself."

"So, how can you help me?"

"Well Marion, we'll start you on a high dose of steroids, and a course of nonsteroidal immunomodulators to stop the inflammation. Then you'll have external beam radiation therapy, which will cause cataracts, so we'll do the surgery to remove them. After that, we'll begin the orbital decompression surgery, so we'll pop the eyeball out and shave away some of the bone inside the eye sockets..."

I have visions of eyeballs rolling around on the hospital floor. I'm starting to feel physically sick, and he's still talking...

"Then, to realign the eyeballs, we'll do some strabismus surgery. Finally, we can do eyelid surgery to correct the retraction and then cosmetic surgery, and you'll be as good as new!"

He looks so pleased with himself. I want to throw up!

"So... so I need all of this to get rid of double vision?"

"Oh, there's no guarantee it will stop the double vision."

"WHAT!!! No way! No way am I going through all of that if it's not going to fix my vision!" The screaming inside my head is drowning out his words

Can you remember a situation when you have heard some news that you just wanted to run away from? I wanted to get out of there.

I don't remember getting home, or ever crying so much when I got there. I didn't want my eyeball 'popped out', but I didn't want to go blind

Surely there has to be another way? I went in search of alternatives. I had many well-meaning friends and family members telling me what I should do, "Marion, have the operations, take the drugs." I became obsessed. I talked about it all the time, and it started to get me down.

Terence (my loveliest brother) seemed to understand. His big blue eyes full of love and his soft voice caressed my ears, "Marion, you must have heard me talk about Máire? She's helped me so much, I think you might like her, so I've made an appointment for you and she will fit you in tomorrow."

So, the next day you find me lying on Máire's couch:

"You know Marion, your body still knows its original template. It knows what it was like before this condition began, and it can get back there if you're prepared to do what's needed."

Template? I'd never heard anything like that before, did she mean like the original software I used to install into the computers?

Máire was exactly what I needed at that moment. She helped me to realise that I am in control of my body, my thoughts, feelings and emotions. She introduced me to the Emotional Freedom Technique. This had a powerful impact on me, and so I trained as an advanced practitioner. I began to study more and found META-Kinetics, which uses Kinesiology with a deep understanding of the language of symptoms.

While healing myself, I was also able to share it with others, just like I did with yoga.

Like me, many of the people that I started to help were trying to resolve the symptoms and not the cause. I found that a lot of the time, most people delete the pain/problem (not you right, just someone you know!).

How many times have you been able to see someone else's problem, when they themselves are unable to see it?

One such example is when I could see something in someone you already know:

Cheryl Chapman

I met Cheryl as a fellow coach at Andy Harrington's Professional Speakers Academy.

I remember thinking, "How fantastic to meet a kindred spirit. A fellow northerner and a straight talker. WOW, she has an amazing ability to see the essence of others. Listen to her! She is so precise with her feedback, not only on the presentation, but she also appears to have laser-like vision of what was blocking other people from achieving their goals."

We started to work together as speaker coaches, and as I spent more time with Cheryl, I began to sense just how much she was holding herself back. She didn't know she was doing this. She would hide her greatness, shy away from it, shielding herself behind an energetic brick wall that helped her to block out emotions. It was clear that she'd experienced some deep trauma, and had learned very early in life how to protect herself. Isn't it strange how you can see something so obviously in others, and yet you still need others to see it in you?

I knew she was a tough cookie, so if I just blurted out what I sensed she'd just shrug it off, probably deny it and I'd never have the opportunity to see her blossom as I knew she could.

Would you agree that sometimes we have to use alternative ways to help someone?

It's like when you encourage a child to eat by pretending to be a 'Chu Chu Train' or an aeroplane, to deliver some kind of vegetable to your child's mouth. Knowing that Cheryl was a supportive and giving person, I devised a plan:

"Cheryl, I need case studies to complete my Master Practitioner in META-Kinetics, would you mind helping me?"

I knew that if I could help her to see clearly what her unconscious limitations were, this would give her the understanding she needed to become even better at helping herself (and others) to blossom and grow.

So, a few days later, there we were. Cheryl was lying on her back, in the living room of my cluttered flat in Angel Islington. I'm balancing my case study sheets on her body, and I can see her state changing. Her breathing speeds up, and her language has changed too.

Wow, I wasn't expecting that reaction. Ok, I'll just write it down, that's interesting... oh shit the papers keep slipping. Never mind, this is fascinating. She's so close to something really important, let me try to see if this is one of her beliefs.

"So Cheryl, does "I have to be careful around people" mean anything to you?"

Oh yes! Eureka! She is crying, so I know she is connecting to this block.

It's such a powerful moment when you bring an unconscious belief into conscious awareness.

"This is really good Cheryl – crying is the best signal we can have right now."

I'm trying my best not to sound too excited or enthusiastic about her obvious distress, but to me, crying like this is like striking GOLD!

"So Cheryl, if you didn't have to be careful – what would you be?"

"Em...em...em... I don't know...what do you mean, Marion? When you say not being careful it's like you want me to stand in front of oncoming traffic on the M1 motorway!"

Handing her another tissue, "Well, what about carefree Cheryl – how would it feel to be carefree?"

"Marion, I don't know, what does that even mean? Carefree – I don't know what it means, isn't the opposite of careful careless?"

We agreed that 'mindful' was not too different from careful, but meant being more aware.

Since this session I often witness Cheryl checking herself when she's being too careful, and I'm so happy that I got to share this moment with her. A moment when she began to be free from something that she didn't even know was holding her back.

Have you ever had the feeling that you have more to offer? Often, things that happen to us when we are younger are what lead to these limitations. These are situations where, for whatever reason, you may have needed to stay safe. In order to do this, your mind creates a 'strategy' to keep you safe.

In Cheryl's case – being left alone at 5 years old – staying safe was a good strategy. However, as a woman heading towards the age of 50, it was no longer serving her. It's about refusing to accept your fears. It's about refusing to accept your glass ceiling, and never settling for something good instead of something truly great.

It is only through finding my WHY that I have been able to set my intention, discover opportunities and take steps to create the life I have now. My WHY is to find joy, have fun and guide others to join me. It is about helping them to find their own WHY, and having fun in the process.

As human beings, we are social creatures. Being connected to others, and living as part of supportive and nurturing community, is our innate way to feeling part of this world. The more you know about who you are, and what your WHY is, the easier it will be to remove the obstacles that hold you back.

Now you can focus on what you want from life. You can take steps to achieve your success, and allow yourself to be fulfilled, satisfied and happy!

Finding our individual WHYs allowed Cheryl & I to realise that as a team, we can help others in a unique way. What's more, we can do so in a way that enables us not only to Live, Love and Laugh every day, but to help others to choose a life of freedom.

We look forward to helping you Find Your WHY! and in turn, helping you discover what to do with it!

CHAPTER 10

HOW CAN I SUPPORT YOU?

Congratulations, you have reached the end of the book

You might not know this, but by reaching this chapter, you have already put yourself one step ahead of the game. Many people don't ever buy a non-fiction book after school, and even less actually read them. Andy Harrington – my original mentor – calls this 'shelf development'.

By completing this book, I know that you are already on your way to making positive changes in your life, and not just someone who pretends that they want to make a change.

If you haven't already completed the WHY questions from Chapter 8, I urge you to do that now. Why would you want to wait? We all need new strategies for moving

forward, so welcome positive change with open arms. I look forward to reviewing your answers and connecting with you.

I would love to hear your thoughts on this book. If you are generous enough to do so, I will offer a gift to you when you post a review on amazon.co.uk. This gift is a free downloadable copy of my Action Planner, ideal as a way to start putting your newly found WHY into action.

I also welcome your comments on ways that I can support you even further, which will help me to serve you in a way that helps you. Please contact me on any of the below social media sites.

 cherylchapman_    CherylC TV   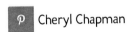 Cheryl Chapman

I have weekly posts on YouTube and Facebook, and so I invite you to subscribe, so that you do not miss any of the interviews or answers to my Follow up Friday videos.

 CherylC TV

If you have any questions that you would like me to answer on the Follow up Friday sessions, please mail me directly on Cheryl@cheryl-chapman.com.

I don't know about you but I really like to meet people face to face. Whilst that is not always possible, it would be great if you could post a picture of yourself with a copy of my book. Each month I'll choose a reader of the month, and you'll receive a surprise gift too – all you need to do is post a picture and call it, 'This is me finding my WHY!'

In closing, I want to say thank you. Thank you for believing in me enough to read this book, but more importantly for believing in yourself. You are a unique, amazing woman and I really hope that our paths will cross again soon.

Please keep me posted on the wonderful things that start to show in your life. I'll leave you with one final story:

When I was 7 years old, my parents bought me tickets to go and see The Osmonds in London (they were like the One Direction of the 70's). Donny Osmond was my favourite.

When the tickets arrived, one of them had a star next to the seat number:

"Mum, why is there a star on my ticket?" (Yes it's the WHY question again)

"I don't know Cheryl, I imagine it is a very special seat."

I decided it was the seat that meant I would be chosen to marry Donny.

When we arrived at the event I was devastated to find that the 'star' just represented the seat at the end of the row.

So, why do I tell you this? Well, it reminds me of the imagination you have as a child, and how disappointments mean that you stop dreaming.

In 2014, I flew to Toronto Canada to talk at an event. I saw a sign that Donny and his sister Marie were in town with their Christmas show.

So, off I went to buy a ticket:

"I'd like the best seat you have please."

"Yes ma'am, we have one right in the centre or there is one here on the end of the row, a little further back."

Which seat would you have chosen?

30 minutes into the show, Donny runs up the aisle and stops right next to the seat on the end of the row.

Guess where I was?

That right, right there.

I stand up and get to hug my idol and then I say, "Donny would you do me the honour of being…in a selfie with me?" (Hey, times had changed in 43 years!)

Here's the interesting thing: I would have never had chosen the end of the row seat if I hadn't had the disappointment 43 years earlier.

In writing this book I also remembered my favorite Donny song was called "WHY"

https://youtu.be/uEZJyfPkWCY

I believe what happens to you in your past is for a reason and in the words of the Osmonds "Let the reason be LOVE!"

https://www.youtube.com/watch?v=_iVWg5T7fXM

Me & Donny Osmond in December 2014

Welcome12X